Alone In Her Presence
Meditations on the Goddess

Erick DuPree

Copyright © 2014 Erick DuPree
All rights reserved.
978-0692220443

*For Goddess,
in whom we live, move, and have our being...*

Starhawk & T. Thorn Coyle, because you taught first…
Yeshe Rabbit Matthews & Crystal Blanton, because of you,
I am no longer alone…

ALONE IN HER PRESENCE

When I'm alone with her
My soul learns worship
In spirit and in truth
Peace fills my heart
Joy reigns and rules there
Nothing but love overflows
And Her truth clearly shown
When I'm Alone in Her Presence

Over the last few years, I have had the fortune and honor to write a very popular blog called *Alone In Her Presence*. Like me, it has gone through many cycles of growth, death, and rebirth. Each year helping me to express to the fullest extend my spiritual experience in devotion Goddess. There where the quiet months wherein I wrote nothing, and the prolific, where it seemed I wrote nearly every day. *Alone In Her Presence* launched me into the Pagan community as a voice. One that over time people began to listen to. I'll never forget the moment when a prominent Pagan sent me a message that said, "call me, we need to talk." In an instant, I became very public, very fast and discovered that life in service to the Goddess is interesting in the Agora.

Along the way, I have made life-changing friendships with people who challenge the way I approach my writing, and how I walk in the world. They've helped me to refine my writer's voice, listen within and to discern, so that I can articulate the stories that most need to be told. When reviewing the blog for this collection, a sort of 'best of', I see my growth but also that I wrote some of my most popular workings on *Alone In Her Presence.* Even now, after archiving *Alone...* and moving on to other writing, I am still delighted to see favorites continue to be be read today.

Today, I am no longer the alone blogger, but rather part of a collective of other Pagan writers. Each of us with a unique voice, brought together in service to bring people into the gathered community of Goddess' love. That community is not just Pagan, or witchcraft, but Buddhist, Tantric, Shamanic, and more. It is from the widest umbrella we experience Goddess.

My blog inspired this little book, however herein contains more than just blog entries. Instead, I offer expanded thoughts on the perennial favorites, perennial favorites, like "Knowing Goddess of Wishful Thinking." These are the writings that made *Alone In Her Presence* the reflection of personal gnosis that grew into public teachings. These are the essays on worship, ritual, and knowing the Goddess, feeling nature, as well as writing on magic making and immanence. I have also included a collection of my unpublished poetry that I have written over the last five years. Some of this poetry later went to inspire ritual; others reflected a certain period of growth. Lastly, there are two rituals on encountering the Goddess. The first is Daily Practice for welcoming the Goddess into your life, and the second, is dedicated to healing from traumatic experiences.

I have intentionally left pages unnumbered, because the journey to Goddess has no beginning and no end. Rather, the story of the Goddess, in Her infinite wonder is one that continues serves as manifold witness. It is not just my journey, but the journey's of many, all whom are seekers of wisdom, power, and love that I dedicate this merit. I endeavor for it to serve.

Blessings,
Erick DuPree
Beltane, 2014

POETRY

MORNING PRAYER

Love is the Spirit of this morning,
and I am Your prayer,
Love is the hope that unites me,
as You remove despair.
Love is universal salvation,
to give me unto this day,
Love is the joy, the breath,
the calm in how I make way.

Love is the magic the bonds us,
from whence I became You
Love leads me back to Center,
it is You whom is true
Love is our bond sacred,
Earth most reverent, holy and compete
Love welcomes morning's perfect and Perfection
welcomes me.

Love, in all ways, always, a love divine.

GREATNESS

I'm safe and sound
Serene and calm
Whenever I'm here, I know she's with me
My secret place
Where I escape
From all the cares of this race
Because of Her grace

The wisdom is served
And life so preserved
All from your words that speak Her
Power displayed
And weakness fades
All of the pain erased
Because of her greatness

Goddess...

...As my Artemis
loves to frolic
by the river
plotting out her hunt

Athena does reside
within me
as moments of
clarity and wisdom
will reveal

My Isis would gladly
search the world over
to put you back
together with her love

When I am calm
and nurturing, well
that's my Madonna moment

Hera shows herself
with the sting of betrayal
stealing Zeus' thunder
when lightning strikes

Hestia resonates and permeates
hearth and home
as fresh bread slowly bakes
over a welcoming fire

Morrigan peaks out
from time to time
with her war and death
as I struggle to make
sense of myself

Ma'et
of course is most elusive
as I attempt to live
wholeheartedly...so you see, I am goddess...

Rainbow

In sunny solitude
The swelling seas
Erase the bank of haze
Birds begin to sing
A skylark soars in the air

Purple hills of paradise
No longer dampened souls
Tossing and turning in the night
Pearl white peaks
Hypnotize across the planet

The color of strength
Of a rainbow myriad
Green cascading canopies
No longer drinking
Nature's tears away

With fluorescent green
Humming birds
Under the turquoise sky
The vintage rustic vines
Are revived to a new life

Rejoicing hearts
Of amethysts and emeralds
Are awakened from
The breeze of heaven

Vines whisper in awe

Her sun
Sky sweet bliss
Fountain overflows
To twilight shade
Robed fields of gold

Her young berries
Plump and iridescent
Until harvest comes
She will say goodbye
And again renew

INFINITELY LOVABLE

In her eyes the starkness of might
in her outstretched arms a call
to the ones challenging her
to surrender to her power
and the ones worshipping her
to find in her might what's hidden,
an invitation to the worshipper and the challenger
to submit, to see, beyond her wrathful might
not a goddess
but a woman, a mortal lover,
infinitely lovable

EARTH MOTHER RISING

From deep within the swirling water her presence came to me,
I embraced her in my arms to feel her eternal warmth,
Her wisdom limitless in the silence of the water,
Her majestic flames encrypted my body,
I can feel the roots of eternity setting in,
Her entity as cold as the night,
Without her we would die,
The Goddess is our mother,
The Goddess is all around us,
The Earth is our mother.

SILVER GODDESS

The storm is coming
Please hunker down
The rain is falling
On the silver goddess crown

Yet she stays there
Stays in the gentle rain
I touch her hair
The silver goddess chain

Yet I stay there
Entangled in the silver chain
And yet I'm dying there
Before the silver goddess feign

Dead, dried lips
Malevolent eyes
Beautiful hips
A perfect disguise

Yet the crown has fallen down
The jester returned to his shell
He's getting out of this town
Because of silver goddess spell

Who Is

Who is the daughter of Artemis.
Hair flowing, arrow soaring, wind rushing.
Fierce, independent, unafraid.
I can do this thing called life.

Who is the sister of Aphrodite.
Sweet kisses, lullabies, passion and envy.
You and me, forever together.
Love is all that matters.

Who is the mother of Athena.
Warrior race, blood spilled, poised to kill.
Wisdom and wit, entwined.
My brains will help me overcome.

I am all goddess unchained.
My enemies should fear me,
my friends surround me,
my lover never leave me.

I will stand unwavering,
my battle cry piercing the air.
My tears will dry themselves.
I need no one.

FERTILITY

You are the life giving goddess
let me fertilize your expectation,
emptying my seed while cupping your richness
and soon your pregnant furrows begin to swell
lush and green.

Feast of dreams, sustenance of my people
your body is a temple giving and giving again.

And when the harvest leaves you barren,
I will let you stretch fallow and rest before
ravishing you and spilling seed once again,
my fingers in your moist darkness,
touching and loving your unselfish giving,

your womb's splendid infusion, corn and wheat
in breezes blowing.   You breathe life into the child
with fierce breasts, your mounds of nourishment.

I bow to your naked purpose proclaiming my
servitude,
tenderly reaping your glorious bounty.

They say
She has an old soul
tried & true
Wrinkled & new
But not worn
Her soul has seen
Many days
And ways
Tripped over puppy love
Let go of silly stuff
Her soul
Has been everywhere
It was meant to be
Now her soul
Has her life to live
Her live to give
her eyes to see
The powers that be
To bring her soul
Back to me
For me to hold
If I may be so bold
Her soul touches me
Gives me light to see
Breathes in my emotion
So I may feel complete
They say she has an old soul
One who already knows
All about me
And the tears I weep

BLOOD MOON

Draw the forces of old and wise peers
From the light of the blood moon.

A lunar eclipse and color radiates
In these consecutive nights.

Energy calls and empowers the bodies
Who call it. The Goddess gives what the
Moon sells to her.

Jai Ma, Kali

Aum Kreem Kalikaye Namaha
Aum Kreem Kalikaye Namaha
Aum Kreem Kalikaye Namaha

I empower Kali to devour the Power
Return it from Darkness to the World as Love

I empower Kali to devour the Oppression
Return it from Darkness to the World as Love

I empower Kali to devour the Prejudice
Return it from Darkness to the World as Love

I empower Kali to devour the Privilege
Return it from Darkness to the World as Love

Aum Kreem Kalikaye Namaha
Aum Kreem Kalikaye Namaha
Aum Kreem Kalikaye Namaha

Aum. Aum. Aum.
As you bow your heart, so I bow to you.
Blessed

BEAUTIFULLY BLIND

it is a quiet afternoon
the weather, the chill is upon my toes
and conditions that have haunted for much too long
have finally realized
windows are alas closed to the distractions of the
street below
but also to the gentle wind that had lightened the room
with its dance
gone

my desk is at a stop
the only sound coming from its viscera is the tapping
my fingers dance on the keyboard of the computer
a cat sleeps at my feet
a telephone silently lies on the table next to me

bored in the melancholic emptiness that is vast as
winter's approach
yet in my mind there is a flurry of activity…

my mind dances one way, stops, looks around,
turns and then dances in a new direction
it skips and runs, then suddenly stops,
confused with it purpose, and its final destination

plays at seeking out the depth of its existence and
when hesitant at its ability to dig into such
insightfulness, shutters and lies down…

unable to justify the journey that it feels is so imperative to take
starts confusion with hysterical obtrusions and innuendos
thoughts with or without intention, straining for reason

all this is mine as i try
sitting in the stillness of my room
to form thoughts into cohesive significance....

in my mind i am beautifully blind

She lies in us all
Connecting
Us to the Earth
Connecting us
With ourselves
Connecting us
To that loving
Caring
Warmth
That intuitive knowledge
Connecting to the spiritual
Connecting to the sensual
Feeling our bodies
Feeling our space
Becoming more open
Truly feeling the love
And the grace
And the warmth
That our mother
Bestows upon all her children
She loves us all
She is willing
To share a little love
With everyone
All you have to do
Is acknowledge her
And the wonderful
Beautiful
And mysterious world
That we all live in

Harvest comes and as the light wanes
The reapers reap, let the bounty be of plenty
Empower us that Love remain the Law
May our rejoicing be in our hearts
May worship be of intention and deed
May we be of community known of Goddess
Let daily Worship be in a Heart that Rejoices

So Mote It Be

This night as the pomegranate ripens
  As the hermit crabs come out of their den and into sand
This night as the spotted egg is released from its wren song
  And as the cherry tree sets down its pink blossoms
  This night as the windows keep promises to open
  As the fire continues to keep its promise to warm

This night as rain leaps to the waiting of roots in their dryness
  And starlight bends to the roofs of the hungry and tired

This night Moon is released from inside the darkness
As someone steps into the light of magick's embrace

> Tonight, let Her light bless you…
> With sacred love, let Her bless you.

Let the vow of this night keep itself…Wildly and wholly,
  Spoken and silent…. Surprise you inside your ears
Sleeping and waking… Unfold it self inside your eye.

> Let Her fierceness and tenderness
> Hold you
> Let Her vastness be undisguised
> In all your days

Movement

There is movement in my life right now…a constant humming of alteration inside and out.
Changes…some voluntary, some unintentional, creating fresh accountabilities, forcing me to balance the ever-present flow of thoughts and actions that are taking place as I evolve into another faze of my existence.
Just when life was safe and known…
Just when I had settled in, to rest, to nest within a comfort zone…
I start to look around, restless and bored, eager to begin passages again…
To know the unknown…
There is movement in my life right now.
I've stirred the pot...
There is nothing more that I can do but settle in among its transformation…
And live within the adaptations of its growth.

Time
You haunt me
Slipping by so silently
Counting as you do
In miniscule amounts amassed
The composition of my life
Today within tomorrows past

Time
What promises we made
What plans we swore to keep
Till you passed faster through my days
Than I dared creep

Days End

The sun is setting in the studio.

A draped figure, a woman's dress-form costumed in a garment designed to fill the humor and the moment of another night, standing tall and silent now a few feet in front of me, is slowly disappearing in the darkening room. The wall clock next to it has not chimed the hour in over a year, has not moved a minute past 7:58, will not, until I choose to bring it back to life again.

Goddesses stand silently on a bookcase. Books are stacked in piles on the floor. Everything in this room was put into it with intention, yet as it all fades into THE ANONYMITY OF THE NIGHT I WONDER WHY…

What need is there in me to pervade upon the uncluttered areas of this studio… and in its empty moments of unproductive time?

Why do I hold on to the past when my reason for existing seems to be only for the future?

What comfort is there in the memories…

ESSAYS

THE LIVING RITUAL OF GODDESS

The Living Ritual of Goddess is not, while it may sound like it, a five-point plan to connecting to Goddess. Rather, it's approaching whatever your daily practice is with realized intention and the ritual rubric: that detailed method of procedure faithfully or regularly followed. Like when we use the athame.

For me, it's waking up every day and making time for Her FIRST! It's intentionally saying the same daily Morning Prayer because that prayer, which I wrote, opens my soul. It's using the same yoga asana in a routine formula that opens my heart with a specific type of advanced yogic breath work. I have ritualized practices for every aspect of Goddess, with the goal to ground and connect myself back into my body and my soul. These are simple, moments to shift conscience at my desk at work, on the subway, in line at the grocery store. I've even done it while "doing it!"

Sometimes we loose the breath. We loose step with the beat. Sometimes gentle reader, we get swept up in a cyclone of emotion and that is when we need the Living Ritual that instantly connects us back to Goddess. Without it, our emotion can lead to unsavory or unsafe places and practices. Ritual gives us the tools to reach for love over hate when our anger frames intention. With it we can find divine perspective, and use our magic to develop negatives into positive pictures.

This is why I create rituals for Daily Practice that ground me back into Goddess should ever I gets lost. And to make sure what I craft is grounded in wisdom, power and love, I do the rituals of Wicca from time to time. This is why I take classes with esteemed teachers of the Golden Dawn. Why I study Tantric Thelema and why I read Marija Gimbutas still. This is why I am a yoga teacher, why I sit in meditation as taught to me through the Soto-Zen lineage, because all these facets of ritual, these processes, this wisdom all connect me back to Goddess.

Together we explored communion, worship, and now Ritual and I wonder where are you on your walk? Let this be an open invitation to explore the walk with Goddess. Whether that walk is exploring a ritual tool like an athame or turning your daily practice into a Living Ritual of Goddess. When we come into Goddess' divine embrace we come into an experience that is undisguised in all Her ways. She is love, and she loves you.

Worship in the Heart that Rejoices

I confess worship is one of my favorite words. But what is worship? When I was growing up my grandmother would say, "Worship is a verb!" Meaning that there was more to being a Christian than just showing up on Sunday morning or worse, just at Christmas and Easter! She is not wrong, as worship is in fact both a noun and a verb.

Worship the action of religious devotion often directed towards a deity.

I've been wondering how we as the beloved community gather in worship. As we enter into the Harvest cycle of our year and many magical things fall into alignment, soon it will be all witches and magic in preparation for Samhain, and our worship will be often on display.
Or will it?

For many, our ritual will be public but is ritual and worship the same thing? I believe that ritual can be part of worship, but that worship is a distinct entity unto itself in communion with Goddess, whether alone or in a group.

At it's core worship is about worth, our worth and Goddess. As you know, I believe strongly in the immanence of divinity, and thus I tie worth directly to deity. But did you know that worship the word, is derived from the Old English worthscipe, meaning worthiness or worth-ship—to give, at its simplest, worth to something. One of the things at drew me into Goddess was an overwhelming sense of worthiness within Her presence. Before I was alone in her presence, I felt hopeless. Before I felt Her divine embrace and understood that interconnectedness, I felt worthless. But knowing Goddess, and being connected to a spiritual community that lifts up instead of shames were life saving.

Within the Goddess community, the Pagan community I discovered that being different was ok. I learned that sex was sacred, and not just one kind of sex for example but all acts of love and pleasure. I came to experience that we as a community strive to be authentic, and honor our success and failures, as we lift each other up. I discovered my voice, and most importantly, I learned and continue to learn how to use my voice and magic to help others. Because living within the Goddess is ultimately not about what spell I do or don't do, but the intention I bring to the magic I make. That relationship with you, with myself and with Goddess is all about honoring inherent worth.

Recently, I was asked how do I worship the Goddess? I worship the Goddess first by actively engaging in the inherent worth within Goddess herself. Meaning, I LIVE a life devoted to Goddess. Devoted to the principles ascribed to the Earth as her vessel, to the life forces that are within the vessel and to the vessel that contains Her divine magic. I do this because I make Love the Law. I do this because I live according to a Dharma principle of walking authentically. And, I know I do this correctly when I whisper words about her endlessly, in spiritual communion with Her and the spirit guides.

The Charge of the Goddess mentions worship once. "Let my worship be in the heart that rejoices." Following this is "all acts of love and please are my ritual." Many people quote the all acts of love and pleasure part of the Charge, as it affirms many marginalized people, and rightly so. However, Henry Ward Beecher, is quoted as saying, "I never knew how to worship until I knew how to love." It seems Love and Worth and Goddess is the rubric for a heart that rejoices. The divine embrace of the Great Mother is the refuge for patriarchy's battered children, where worship has not been about giving worth. The Goddess leads us back into self, and into our inherent worth, and deeply into Her. It is there we find hope and transformation for each other and for tomorrow.

GODDESS AS SPIRITUAL COMPANION

You know, I whisper words about Her endlessly. I see Goddess everywhere I go, and in everything I do. How can I not? Much can be said about archaeologist Marija Gimbutas' Language of the Goddess, but this is fact, "The world of the Goddess implies the whole realm in which She manifested herself!"

I am the Goddess, you are the Goddess, and we are the Goddess... This is the great interconnectedness that makes today's modern Paganism something more than just a religion in the orthodox way contemporary liturgist, e.g. monotheistic define religions. Together we are on a journey to discover, to feel and to know and to live and love. But also to push, to shape and to change as Crowley once said, the art and science of change is magic.

As I come to know myself, I trust in a walk that goes deeper into Goddess because we are companions, She and I, on a spiritual quest. But what does that mean?

Goddess for me is not omnipotent. I do not see Her through the same lens as Christians may see their God. This is an important distinction to make. Goddess is not 'looking down upon me from the heavens'. Goddess as I know Her isn't my savior, and I am not waiting for redemption. I have not done anything 'wrong'. Often a stumbling block for people new to modern Paganism is unlearning the patriarchal paradigm. It takes time, but it happens. Goddess worship does not hold the same belief tests for entry, and blessed be for that!

Rather, for me, I am enveloped within Goddess. I live within Her as Earth, and breath Her and exhale Her. I drink Her and excrete Her. I am built from Her and make love in a manner affirmed by Her, because She made it so. I was born of the Earth and I will return of the Earth, and so Earth will do the same. And we each hold a part of that cycle. But we also hold other planes both physical, emotional, and psychic, all interconnected. Woven into a journey. Through out those journeys over millennium Goddess came to be known by many names and many faces and all genders. However, for me ultimately She is essentially the energy that sustains life.

Goddess is wisdom, and that wisdom's gives life it's shape. She is the answer and the question. Which sounds wonderfully beautiful as I write it, and also like an obnoxious enigma, I know. Much of what is written, even Doreen's Charge of the Goddess is 'enigmatized' and shrouded in occult mystery. In this day it need not be. Actually, Goddess as your spiritual companion is exactly whom you need Her to be as you are, with perfect love every time you whisper Her name. It really is that simple, as simple as whispering Her name. Good Morning Goddess…

Each morning, I wake up and I call Her name. Not out loud, but as I roll over and look out my urban window at a not so magical view, I whisper Good Morning. I acknowledge Her first. I think with reverence that She is with me. Sometimes She is just divine energy, sometimes She is the face of the horned God, and my beloved and I go to work with a smile on our face. Other times She is the face of another Goddess, maybe Innana, with a different message. Sometimes She's the alarm clock, and "Oh Fuck…I'm gonna be late!" But regardless, I take a moment first for Her. I honor Her and in turn She honors me.

That is the dance of companionship. I'm never truly alone, because I am with her. Even when I was small and sore afraid, I had Her. And so do you. I believe that making time for Goddess, as Spiritual Companion is the single most important thing you can do on you journey. When we make time for Her, we are forced to make time for ourselves with daily practice.
To go back to that Charge:

She has been with us from the beginning, and she is that which, is attained at the end of desire.

Those are truly words to live by.

Knowing Goddess, Or Just Wishful Thinking?

"Have you experienced visions or dreams… maybe voices, or other mystic phenomena related to the Goddess?" That was recently asked of me.

It got me to thinking, when had Goddess appeared before me? I mean really appeared, and given me direction or information via visionary or auditory means? And if She did, how was I to know when my mystical experiences are actual gnosis versus imagination or wishful thinking? What makes experiences of the Goddess REAL?

It was such a great question, which had me meditating about experiences and connection to Goddess and others. We live in a society that seems to really empower the "I feel" statement. Framing things with "I feel" has a nicer ring to it, and I agree that often it is the better model. However, the "I feel" doesn't always equate to fact or knowing. So how do we know when Goddess is speaking, and are we listening?

Last March, when I was sculpting an image of Goddess at Ostara, as I was working the pigments of colors into the wet clay I had a vision inside the clay of a friend whom I had not talked to in almost a year. This was a friend I had been very close too, and for whatever reason, mostly busy schedules and a change in jobs, we had drifted apart. As I was sculpting, which is by nature ritualistic for me, I saw my friend having an abortion. Let me be clear in this, I saw exacting details that need to be recounted here.

As I came out of the vision, chilled and frankly disturbed I didn't know what to do? So, I texted that random "Thinking about you" and let her know that I felt she needed to know she wasn't alone and I loved her. Random huh? She ignored me. What else could I do? She and I were not close any more but where still connected. I sent healing energy her way and placed her on my altar and into my stream of consciousness. I never forgot the vision, and never parted with the art.

She contacted me a month ago that she was moving, and we had drinks two weeks ago. Over drinks it was like we had never missed a beat. She told me how she and her husband had split, how she cheated and she had to made bad choices. She then told me about the abortion. All in a bar, a nice bar mind you, and how I texted the night she had the procedure. She asked how I knew. It was time, and finally that I wasn't just "plain old Erick." then she understood why my counsel was always the one she sought.

Some might consider that vision a psychic connection, and not a Goddess connection. I could argue either point. However I feel strongly because the vision happened at Ostara, a time of great fertility, while I was aspecting Goddess through art, there was a deeper message; one meant for me and a message for my friend. For me, it was a reminder of duty to Goddess and to my role as teacher and counselor and for my friend, well that is between her and Goddess. That is just one of many examples I have of connection to Goddess.

Connection is about the realness in the moment. On Ostara, I set out to sculpt a Goddess I intended to donate to a fundraiser for The New Alexandrian Library Project. That was my plan. Goddess however had a different plan. I was not prepared and quite frankly desirous of that transmission. It wasn't pleasant to say the least. I had to learn to understand it, ground myself with it, and then release it; in addition to attempt to heal a person I cared for, who did not on the surface want my company in that moment.

Which leads me to this thought on real verses wishful? I think for me, the realness comes because I set intention to not seek "fantastical" Goddess experiences. I am not looking for Goddess to magnify Erick, and Goddess knows, She certainly doesn't need me to magnify Her. I am not, to quote Tibetan

Buddhist nun, Pema Chödrön, biting the hook that leads to suffering or dukkha. Instead, I choose to align a life dedicated to Goddess and creating magic that works towards systemic changes for positive good of all beings in the world. I come to Goddess knowing She is the bringer of wisdom in Her time, and I invite Her, entreat upon Her to use me as a vessel.

Because of that, She honors many, not just me with Her wisdom and speaks knowingly and I listen. I listen in the trees and I listen in the wind. I listen in the laughter of children and in the faces of friends and strangers. I see Her in visions but I see also in the reality of life's struggles. I know Her in the morning and evening star. However, I know Her best within myself, for it is She who called upon my soul to arise and come unto Her.

She has been with us ALL from the beginning and she is that which is attained at the end of desire.

GODDESS IMMANENT

I have been exploring various religions, faiths, and their many praxis of belief for a long time. Having been reared in orthodoxy, I have come a long way from conservative, stumbled a moment at atheist (really agnostic but at the time atheist sounded avant garde, no?) to Zen and paganism and finally into self. Recently I was reading Sam Webster's account on paganism, idolatry and the restoration of pagan experience and I began to ask myself "what do I believe?"

Really what I have been questing for was interconnectedness with divinity. Often in my writing and my practice I use the expression, "Goddess that flows in, among, and around us." I first heard this phrase from a teacher, T. Thorn Coyle several years ago. Over the years, as I have gone deeper and without the limitations of paganisms label; e.g. Feri, Wicca, Thelema; I came to understand that to mean "flowing in, among, and around us" as Immanence. It was Phyllis Curott who first introduced me to the word immanence in her book WitchCrafting. Immanence isn't a word we hear often, and certainly not within pagan writing. Immanence, like other heavier religious vocabulary (theurgy comes to mind), doesn't come up in many pagan writing, although I suspect many come into presence through Immanent experiences.

Immanence refers to philosophical and metaphysical and metaphysical theories of divine presence in which the divine is seen to be manifested in or encompassing the material world. This is contrasted to transcendence, in which the divine is seen to be outside the material world. Most Christian faiths, "god" is outside the body, in heaven looking down upon you. God the omnipresent and omnipotent, opposed to a more matriarchal view that Goddess is part of the collective whole. I think many, myself included for years, continued to dwell in transcendent understanding of divinity when applied to Goddess based faith practices.

The more I come to know Goddess and come into direct relationship with Her, the more I come to believe that Transcendent divinity is a patriarchal construct. The idea that the divine is separate from us, and in some way controls us into subjugation doesn't sit well with my understanding of an all loving and all encompassing divinity that magic makers work with. My relationship with Goddess is not suppliant but instead a partnership in the interconnected wellness of community.

For me, the 'divine' is experienced as Goddess is in the totality and expression of a collective and interdependent divine energy that "flows in, among, and around each of us." And thus though that lens, my reverence is for all and everything. On the surface, it might sound a bit arrogant, that I would consider myself divine. "Do you see yourself as a God?" Yes, I see myself as a walking reflection of Her most divine nature. The shadow and the light, all encompassing. Sometimes I struggle and sometimes I succeed, but its always in direct relationship to how I walk my path with others, in Immanence. There is no promise of eternal sunshine and constant ease in any divinely inspire text, from the Vedas to the Bible. But there is devotion. For me that is devotion to Goddess, Self, and All.

So, here we are with one Goddess within over one God above, but it is not that cut and dried and not nearly so monotheistic as it sounds. Firstly, why Goddess? Because all life is born of the female, and through that birth comes rebirth. All Goddess cultures come into birth and rebirth via this known truth. Whether ancient like Shakti or modern like Feri's Star Goddess, it is through the female that the first concept of life emerges. It is from this interconnected divinity, that when I say immanent divinity, I am really saying that I am Goddess, you are Goddess and that all is Goddess. And in the totality that is Goddess, nothing is Goddess also.

"But what about Hekate, Isis, or Aphrodite, and where

is the masculine?" This is where I sometimes find myself at times at odds with others within my community. This is because before all other deities of many names, faces and personalities, I call upon Goddess Immanent first. As the primal life force that is everything and nothing at the same times, I honor Her and myself first in all ritual and workings, but also in daily practice. It is only upon honoring the Immanent love that is She, that I enter in communion with any other given deity. In practice this looks like calling upon Goddess as Holy Mother first and then welcome the elements and finally I invite the presence of the gods whom will aid me on my journey. To me, they are like old friends, teachers, and guides, each special and unique to the magic I am doing and towards the greater fulfillment of Immanence. Like me, these holy deities are also part of Immanence.

It was Joseph Campbell who said, "It is mankind that gives God a face." Depending on where I am, I may spend months with a Goddess like Kali, or challenge myself in getting to know the Horned God. It is the purest form on polytheism, aligning with the interconnectedness that is all the gods in the panoply of polytheism. Sometimes, there is no deity practice beyond Earth. Just me and the dirt and Immanence. Someone once asked me to describe the Goddess, and I said, "She is the purest energy and form, all resonating energy, that is all genders and polarities within my presence."

Because Paganism has no litmus test of belief entry, we all must reconcile how we come to know deity. For me when it comes to Goddess, She who is everywhere, everything, and within everyone. What is it for you?

On Making Magic

The word "magic" derives via the Latin magicus, borrowed from Ancient Greek μαγικός (magikos), originating from μάγος (magos, "wise man, mage"), and as a noun typically means influencing the course of events by using mysterious or supernatural forces. Supernatural forces, makes me think of Hollywood movies and TV!

I prefer to see magic as a verb, to move, change, or create that, which is seen, and unseen. Naturally, one could write a thesis just on the etymology of the word magic, let alone the practical application of it. I am sure there are some great scholarly works? But doubtful, because magic is too broad a topic. I am fascinated most by magic as a tool for personal gnosis, more than it's living history. Yet historically and unfortunately, magic is most commonly seen though centuries of patriarchy and prejudice and is often called witchcraft. But being a witch and practicing magic are not mutually exclusive, for even those who persecuted witches for millennia, practice magic. Not to be glib, but it doesn't get more magical than Pope Patriarchy's transubstantiation! (It wasn't glib until I modified the noun with Pope Patriarchy, but lets face it, I gotta call it like I see it!)

However, what magic actually is is really simple. In one sentence simple. Magic is the ability to create what you seek through your desire and will. This is often called "manifestation through energy and intent" a phrase found in almost every new age book on the application of magic. Magic effects reality in ways that are not fully understood by science, this doesn't make it supernatural, it makes magic different. However, for those who practice magic we fully invite the experienced of 'different' as we invite its practice. The principles of magic are found in positive thinking, manifestation, affirmation, and creative visualization. In many ways, The Secret, the phenom book Oprah shouted about for a moment, put magic in everyone's hands. Even Eckart Tolle's The Power of Now, invites magic and it couldn't be any farther from supernatural.

Magic as I practice it works best when reinforced by action and power for magic comes from the earth, the spirit, and me. My application of magic is part of my ritual communion and connection with Goddess and community. This is because one informs the other. I suppose this makes me a mage, or wise man, or dare I say it; witch! Yet just because I make magic sacred, doesn't mean everyone does. Some might consider if we used the Judeo-Christian paradigm that Magic replaces prayer in witches liturgy and ritual. However while magic and prayer are similar, in that both call on personal and divine power to change the world, the big difference is in how the two call on the divine. Most prayer calls on a god or goddess to change reality for the prayer. Magic calls on the divine to supplement or enhance the power of the caster. Magic encourages closeness and equality with deity, while prayer encourages a certain degree of separation.

Magic has many names, from sorcery to hoodoo, magick with a "c" and a "k" (courtesy of Alister Crowley's Thelema) and even, yes witchcraft. Speaking of Crowley, his definition of magic to me remains evergreen, "The Science and Art of causing Change to occur in conformity with Will". It is this will that makes magic in all forms, the personal power that is infused the intent and then released. There are many magical forms, from simple folk magic to the complex and formal ceremonial magic, but all engage the intent and then release it.

With the definition by Crowley, I am sure many think that all magic is magic. This may be true, but not all magic is the right magic for you. This is because like all things, if magic is part of the journey towards personal gnosis, and hopefully every experience is, then magic is intimate and the discovery of the right blend of magic takes exploration. In order for your magic to work, magic must resonate with the individual performing it. When we send out magic, we also must understand that we receive magic too. It is a circle, and who we are in the spectrum of magical practice is something that is ever evolving, because magic is living. Ultimately, it is about that which you seek, and honoring the practice that works for you.

My steps in magic continue to be first steps, because as I raise palms to the universe and invoke magically, I am constantly reminded that I am but a piece of cosmic wonder in the living ritual that is my magical journey. From simple candles to complex castings; to mantra, mediation, yoga, even sex it is all magic. For me the study of the process of making the magic is just as much part of the magic making. Testing and exploring magic, magic invites a deeper understanding of the energies that dwell within the earth, within each other, and within all beings. I find magic to be one of the keys to unlocking a deeper and more profound experience of being awake.

DREAM GIVER CALLING

There is a story about a girl of the indigenous regions of the Americas, about 17 years old, forced to choose between two courses in life. The one her Father has decided for her "steady as the beating drum" where all her dreaming comes to an end, and the other what her destiny might be if she waits for the Dream Giver to come. In the story she consults the Great Tree for wisdom, and ultimately must decide by the sounds of drums of war, where she will stand when the lines are drawn. When the Dream Giver finally offers her the clear path, she chooses her people as their shaman, over a lover and a new world.

This of course is Disney's retelling of Pocahontas. I recognized then, that Pocahontas, through the lens of animation, was liberally adapted. It is important to openly honor that the Powhatan Nation, have not been honored in their legacy, fiscally or righteously. Their Pocahontas is actually Mataoka whom later becomes Rebecca Rolfe. Her truth can be found in many place. Disney's story should have been simply called Colors of the Wind.

That is the story I love. The story with the life saving messages that honors the Earth, the divine spirit Dream Giver, and the unity of people coming together despite differences choosing Love as Law over the drums of War. Where a princess heard the call of the Dream Giver, and the divine energies of the Earth. Where every rock and tree and creature, had a life, had a spirit, had a name.

I too was once 17 years old and also deciding my density, wrestling with my father, my fate, and my fears. I too felt something more when I touched the rock, the river, and the tree. While they did not "glow" like in the movie as I touched them, I felt the nature spirits everywhere inhabiting the energies of nonphysical worlds, these colors of the wind.

There I found myself deeply called out of the patriarchy of Christianity and my father's house and into nature. Into the wild heart that rejoiced and into an anointed reality of the interconnectedness essential in all living things, where spirits were involved in every aspect of life and in every natural process.

The Dream Giver breathed life into the plants, animals, and human beings each of us made of the four elements; each of us comprised of spirits of earth, air, fire and water. Here within I came into a sacred embrace. Into nature, I discovered a place where every rock and tree and creature of the world was alive, and where life had potential. How high did the sycamore grow? I knew that to cut it down, I would never know. To cut me down I too, would never grow. From depths of the ocean caresses, out sacred healing waters that helped my suicidal younger self. From within the Earth I found myself sacred and reborn.

It was in this grove that when I encountered craft traditions through Starhawk's *The Sprial Dance*, I already understood Immanence of Divinity, that I am Goddess, you are Goddess, we are Goddess. When I read the Charge of the Goddess, I had already met Goddess as Dream Giver. Today she is Great Mother, She is Goddess. She is inseparable from the Earth because She has been a part of the planet Earth for as long as it has existed and will continue to govern until its eventual end. She is the Earth itself, and like all physical matter, evolves spiritually and emotionally with us to manifest great rising tides of change.

Goddess gives wind the colors so that we can paint with the magic of Love in harmony within the great circle of life. When I am lost I connect back to Earth. At 17, I did not know where the path might lead; I just knew that it wasn't the one I was on. The journey was and continues to be fascinating, and like the song, part of a dynamic circle and hoop that never ends . Goddess' emanations oversee all Earth processes. Her great consciousness encompasses every particle of the Earth. She knows even the smallest events. She governs every process of birth, life, and death. She wields the great manifestations of creation because

She is Creation. At the present level of the Earth's development, She emanates balance through the rhythmic nature of the cycles and seasons and through the constant renewal of life. Every Rock and Tree and Creature, even you and I, has a life, has a spirit, has a name; are each an aspect of Her expression of life.

Today, my body is revolting from the bondage that is commercialism, just as I turned away from the bondage of my fathers house when I was 17. My heart is being called. Called back to Earth, and deeper into the manifestation of the truest forms of indigenous, from the Latin root to be within. I am drawn away from, and am disenchanted by the glossiness of many NeoPagan experiences of which, I find them vulgar. I crave instead the vulva of the deep, lush, and fluid Earth. I am pulled into the rhythmic currents of the tide, the sweeping current of nature, the pulsating rhythms where my magic is not in a cast iron cauldron or a besom by my side, but rather my hands in the dirt. I fall back into this simple lesson of that movie, and remembering that every rock and tree and creature has a life and spirit and name. I and find that I speak their names. I speak your name. I speak our name. I speak Her name. Love.

Today, I endeavor a life where the Rock, the River, and the Tree magnify our soul when we sit by them. Where we feel intensified by the Earth's great flow that is more than masculine and feminine, and decidedly perfection in simply being undisguised in every way. Moments when our heart is gloried by the vibrations we feel when we lean against the sacred tree and whisper good morning.

When we walk and the warm breeze tickles me and the rain comes down. I call out and upon our magic that comes alive by fire with heart racing, by the visions I have of Earth's divine transcendence from gentle stream into cataclysmic destruction.

This day, into the empowered moment of surrender, I lean into the Divine wisdom of Earth. As the world grows uneasy and we as people look to make change, and wonder, "What can we do?" I am reminded back to that movie. I am called back into Earth, and the life saving message of Shamanic experience. Today, I consult the sacred tree in my life. I go to the altar of my heart and Dream Giver is calling me back to never ending lesson has stayed with me always…

> You can own the Earth and still,
> All you'll own is earth until
> You can paint with all the
> colors of the wind
>
> The Earth says Heal.
> The Earth says Heal me
> The Earth says Heal each other
> Dream Giver is calling will you answer?

SPEAKING OF THE TREE: GOOD MORNING

I take public transit to work. My office is little over a quarter mile from my house. I don't own a car, never have. My two feet and public transit have always been part of the way I contribute to reducing my carbon footprint. It's one of my many drops in the bucket toward a better world. On the corner of 11th and Walnut Street situated right next to the traffic light, there is a tree and every morning, Monday through Friday, I touch that tree with my left palm as I exit the back of the bus.

I look forward to this tree. He and I have been communicating for over a year since I started taking this route to work. He is waiting for me when I get off the bus. It all began actually, when the bus door clipped my foot while precipitously taking off and the tree broke my fall. Naturally, for the next few weeks I'd tap the tree in an almost "high five" style. But as I became more familiar with the tree, my palm lingered longer and longer. Now, I practically leap out the bus and almost hug him. Yes, the tree is a "he."

It's interesting, the tree and I! I've had this ironic relationship with trees my entire life. I climbed in the trees like I think most children do. I read books in the trees. I loved the leaves in autumn, and would preserve them and make art with them. Unlike other children, I was horrified by Shel Silverstein's book The Giving Tree. I had vicious nightmares and I vowed once I became an educator never to teach that book, and solemnly never have. My exploration of trees fascinated me. They still do. I continue to image entire fairy realms living inside trees with magical doors and portals.

Throughout my formative years, my summers where spent at Gander Brook Christian Camp in Maine, where my father was lead minister and my mother was the camp nurse (talk about nuclear). The only peace I found was in the Birch Grove Chapel, which was an outdoor chapel in a grove that was comprised of only Birch trees. There I would sit in seclusion for hours, and since I was the anointed child of the lead minister and the camp nurse, not one camp counselor dared report me. From age 6 until I turned 17, I spent most summers alone with books or writing, just the Birches and I. I read Wicca for the Solitary Practitioner there, (Oh the books one can cover in other book's dust jackets!), received my first kiss (how he broke enterprise with me, but everyone knew) and lost my virginity (Like a Prayer style…'nuff said!). I got baptized one Sunday morning to shut them up, and aspected the Goddess that same Sunday night sky clad…all in the Birch Grove.

Ha, in retrospect when I look back on those years, I think what endeared me to say, Disney's egregiously poor reconstruction of history of Pocahontas was Grandmother Willow! The shamanism and Earth as spirit is about all they got right! The relationship to trees in my magical journey has always continued to bring me back to center. For example, a few years ago I was feeling a sense of spiritual emptiness. I had amassed a knowledge base around magic and craft and felt I "assimilated it" but had not lived it. I had the swag from the shops but not the due diligence to use any of it. I was spiritually disconnected.

And so I turned to Unitarian Universalism, and with my Master's in Comparative Literature and Religious Studies I was an intellectual shoe-in! I had more vocabulary than Merriam Webster on a collision course with Oxford! I boxed up the swag and set myself on a new spiritual quest. But it didn't last long. About a year in my third eye needed to interpret the swirls of paint, the coffee grinds and soon enough the tarot deck was out. But I was determined… until I saw it. The tree.

On an early Sunday morning, I was on my way to Arlington Street Church, to teach a lesson about Goddess and creationism though the lens of "Earth Based Spirituality" when I walked across the Boston Common and immediately I saw her, this tree. Wind and rain after a nasty storm had rendered her badly battered, and yet in her chaos she had left me the most perfect gift. Clear on my path was a perfectly formed wand of willow, 3/4 the bark stripped off. The tree had once again caught me, and embraced me, and given me something. That wand, a tool for magic I had never really felt 'drawn to' before is my most cherished magical possession today. It is a tool I use frequently, it is possibly the most magical item I own, and importantly for me it came from the Earth directly at a time when the Earth knew I needed it. This is how I know Goddess and magic is real.

But back to the tree on the corner when I get off the bus! For me, being a witch is not about being on display. That is not my style. I was not looking for a tree ritual in downtown Philadelphia, but I was
In need of something to connect me back to nature in a city that is void of much humanity. While every day starts with a Morning Meditation and candle offering to Goddess and many evenings end with Vesper Prayers, the simple practice of touching the tree, followed by touching myself sets Good Morning into motion by rooting me back into humanity.

This act is so simple!

I touch the tree, I bless the tree, I thank Goddess, and I say Good Morning and feel him come alive. Then I touch my chest, I bless myself, I thank Goddess and feel myself come alive… and I say Good Morning.

My tree centers me back to Earth in an urban chaos that is void of much of nature and the humanity that nature reminds us of. That centering awakens me and alerts me to Goddess as the breath of nature and grounded into my body. It is in the relationship with the tree, that I know magic is occurring every morning in a profoundly subtle way.

Magic is an intentional act. It is something we do to create a desired effect. I touch the tree, I bless the tree, I thank Goddess, and I say Good Morning. I touch myself, I bless myself, I thank Goddess, and I say Good Morning. Rinse, Wash, Repeat. 5 days a week.

But I have learned is that spiritual acts sometimes have a way of making themselves known in our lives even if we are not looking for them. I know that the Tree Spirits placed that Birch Grove Chapel as sanctuary to shield me from what could have been many ugly summers. I know that storm happened and that branch was there for a reason. That particular tree was there, minding his business when I fell into him. He graciously caught all 6'5" of me. Together we have developed a bond and I have come to better understand the importance of dedicated spiritual practice through our relationship.

And so, I wonder what is you morning commute? How do you invite the morning into your life and say hello? For me, it has become deeply connected to my special tree. I know that in this moment on the journey Goddess put the tree in the circle of our shared life to ground me, and therefore that is his purpose with me, and my purpose is to use that centering to advance humanity. This is why I touch the tree! I'd love to invite you to comment below and share what you do to ground and center, and welcome the morning.

Tonight I am grateful, and think to Dr. Angelou who said, "They hear. They all hear the speaking of the Tree…"

Blessed Be.

Luna Curativa

For thousands of years, the very first forms of magic were healing magic. Healers used the energies and properties of our great Earth to bring the ailing back into a state of health and peace. While the Sun propagated the land with harvest, they observed that all living things responded to the waxing and waning of the Moon.

During the Full Moon shellfish are plumper and more succulent, and mammals have more blood in their bodies and stronger heartbeats. Women tend to menstruate during the New Moon and ovulate during the Full Moon. The herbs used by ancient healers were said to be best when picked during a particular phase of the Moon.

I am a practitioner of magic, and have studied magical botany and herbalism for the treatment of family. I have found the Moon to be a powerful healing ally. Unlike my healing predecessors of ancient times, I am spoiled by a ready supply of prepared herbs. Therefore, I don't always have to spend a lot of time picking my herbs during the optimal phase of the Moon. However, I have found using herbal therapies in harmony with the phases of the Moon to be a very powerful healing strategy.

Waxing Moon

The waxing phase of the Moon is the best time to build the body up. This is when I use nurturing herbs and tonics to strengthen the body's natural immunities. Raspberry leaf is an excellent tonic for reproductive organs; hawthorn berries are good for the cardiovascular system; nettle is a great blood tonic; marshmallow root is a soothing tonic for the urinary tract; astragalas is a wonderful immune system tonic; burdock is a good liver tonic; red clover builds fertility; oat straw is good for the nervous system; and alfalfa is a fantastic all-around nutritive tonic.

These herbs are simple and gentle. They are best taken in a cup of tea, three to five times a day. During the waxing phase, I also like to increase water intake to avoid water retention. The more water we ingest, the less water our bodies attempt to retain.

This is also a good time to apply medicinal salves and to take therapeutic baths. Most importantly, I work during the waxing Moon to ensure that the body has all the nutritional support it needs. This is the body's building time, and it needs a good supply of minerals, vitamins, carbohydrates, lipids, and amino acids to be healthy. I would also not attempt to fast or to lose weight during the waxing Moon.

Use energy healing techniques to strengthen and reconnect with the earth. Be careful to ground and center when healing so that you never use up your own life force energy. The universe if full of energy to use, and by tapping into it you will be able to help many more people than you could by using just your energy alone.

Full Moon
The Full Moon lasts about three days. It is a very intense phase. Many women still ovulate with the Full Moon. This is the time when I apply the most powerful herbs. I like to use cayenne capsules to treat infections of any kind. Goldenseal is a well-known herbal antibiotic. Echinacea and Lomatium are antiviral. Dong quai, black cohosh and chasteberry are excellent herbs for female hormonal fluctuations.

Energy healing work during the Full Moon is very powerful. On the energetic level, it acts like a magnifying mirror. The strong lunar energy pulls everything out of hiding and reflects it back at us. This is often the time during an acute illness when people feel their worst. The Full Moon intensifies whatever else is going on. Often people aren't even aware that they're sick until the Full Moon hits.

This is also an excellent time for psychological therapy. Emotions seem closer to the surface than usual and social inhibitions melt away. Agendas that have been simmering under the surface tend to come out under the light of the Full Moon. This is a time to strengthen relationships and reaffirm bonds. Never underestimate the healing power of simply holding someone's hand and listening. This is not the time for isolation or introspection. The Full Moon draws all of life toward it. Even the solid ground rises several inches when the Full Moon passes overhead!

Waning Moon
The Waning Moon is the best time to employ therapeutic fasts. I avoid drastic fasting. There is usually no need to starve the body to heal it. However, I found it helpful to limit my intake to juices and soups for a few days during the waning Moon, particularly when I was struggling with the flu. I like to use purifying herbs in moderation at this time. Sage, ginger, lemon, thyme, lavender, and peppermint are all cleansing the clearing herbs.

The Waning Moon is also a good time to do sweats and diaphoretic (sweat producing) baths. In addition, if I were trying to kick a habit, I would do it during the waning phase. Full body massages help circulation and strengthen the eliminative systems. Use energy healing techniques to server unhealthy bonds and strengthen boundaries.

Dark Moon
The Dark Moon is as powerful in its own way as the

Full Moon. It is a time for taking stock. It is a phase of hibernation, retreat, and contemplation. Avoid crowds and gatherings and seek a little time for yourself. Unless an illness is at a critical phase, I frequently cease all therapies for a day or so and allow the body to seek its own level. Rest is crucial during the New Moon. Simple foods and quiet times are powerful healers.

Many women menstruate with the Dark Moon. It is natural to want to curl up in bed with a good book and nice cup of chamomile tea. Stronger nervines (relaxing herbs) are skullcap, hops, catnip, oatstraw and valerian.

After the Dark Moon ends and that first crescent appears, then the healing lunar cycle begins all over again. Most acute illness, like the common cold do not last a full lunar cycle.

•

As I stated in the beginning, I am not a formal herbal practitioner, and by no means is the information here within the definitive guide. Rather a starting point, as it is always wise to consult with your health care provider when experiencing any illness or discomfort.

The information here is culled from sources and my own personal experience. I grow many of my own herbs or purchase from people respected within my close herbal community.

In knowing the Moon, I have come to know my body. Awareness of the rhythms of nature has truly assisted me in formulating the best self care practices to making me a better overall practitioner of magic. That all said, I am also a firm believer in all all magic, including Penicillin, M.D. if needed, so naturally, some conditions will require that you apply therapies that don't necessarily "fit" with the phase of the Moon.

Ultimately, when I make time for the Moon, I am making time For Goddess, and the reflection that is Her. The reflection that is myself. I am making time for me. In a chaotic world when there is little time to take a moment to breathe, I can take a moment for a sip of tea, lean on my fire escape, and gave at the Moon in all her resplendent glory and be thankful for they cycle of renewal that She guarantees every 29.5 days.

RITUALS

Daily Practice

A ritual is ceremony in which actions are performed in a specific order in order to achieve a goal. A simple ritual is getting up in the morning and drinking tea, coffee or water as you read or journal. Ritual is also the space from which Shaman's cure disease and through which many major rites of humans are experienced. It is this regularity and order that creates room for the sacred to emerge. Ritual as both a ceremony and a daily practice is a creative act, which when done with intention and awareness of the present moment is an opportunity to connect deeply with spirit. When you transform your day into a series a rituals that you complete, each with the intention of bringing you closer to spirit, your daily life will transform.

The Power of the Ritual

Spiritual rituals help to strengthen and support your soul and to clear and open your mind to higher guidance. The aim of spiritual rituals is to bring your body and mind into a deeper connection with your spirit every moment of every day. Just as regular practice of physical activities can strengthen your body, regular connection to your spirit through daily rituals can give you spiritual strength. The more time you spend interacting with your spirit, the stronger your relationship with your highest self will be.

Bringing an awareness of spirit into every aspect of your day through ritual leaves you more relaxed, grounded, spiritually connected, nourished, and purpose-driven. Rituals help bring greater mental clarity, physical awareness and emotional stability.

Aligning Your Rituals with the Divine

Think of every regular daily experience as an opportunity to create a ritual. You can create a ritual for cleaning, a ritual for writing, a ritual for bathing, a ritual for eating. If you spend some time to create a small altar for each ritual you want to begin, you can use this altar as the focal point when you begin your ritual. For a ritual to be in alignment with the divine, three qualities are necessary:

1.Right-Intention - The beginning of your ritual is the most important time to focus your mind upon your desire and to commit to mental and ethical self-improvement. Think about what objective you wish to achieve with the ritual and create an intention that supports that objective. For my kitchen ritual, my intention is that I be a blessing to my home, and that my thoughts words and actions reflect that. Each time I light my candle, I set the intention with a short prayer that I will be a blessing to my home as I work in the kitchen.

2. Right-Effort - As you move through your ritual, keep the bigger picture in mind. Try to do your very best and when you make a mistake or reach a roadblock, which you inevitably will, let these slow you down and step more deeply into the moment, letting go and opening to divine intervention. If any thoughts enter your mind that are not aligned with your intention, quietly dismiss them, and refocus your efforts on your intention.

3. Right-Concentration - You also need a clear tangible objective for your ritual time. Choose a specific task to work on and a specific time that you have to complete that task. For example when I am in my kitchen, I usually begin my ritual when I have a specific task ahead of me that will take some time. I also might begin my ritual at the beginning of cleaning the entire kitchen. In this case, I will work for an hour and clean as much as I can during that time. Keeping all of your attention on one objective or task at a time helps you to develop inner peace, insight and serenity of mind.

Meditation

The practice of meditation is a practice of clearing your mind in order to bring greater focus to your body, your thoughts and your emotions. Meditation is a mental practice that you can begin practicing in short periods of time throughout your day. Meditation provides time to disconnect from your personal life and creates space to reflect on deeper parts of yourself. Meditation is grounded in the belief that the essence of yourself can be understood from within. The ultimate goal of meditation is to know your spirit as it manifests within you.

Although there are many different types of meditation, I have found that the meditation practice that has been the easiest to integrate into my life has been the practice of mindfulness meditation. Mindfulness meditation is a practice of bringing your full awareness to every moment of your day. You can begin simply by bringing your complete attention to your everyday tasks like brushing your teeth or driving to work. The practice is to simply observe your thoughts and emotions without getting carried away by them. As you practice witnessing yourself, you can begin to detach from the unconscious aspects of your personality as you bring them into full awareness.

I began creating rituals when I first started working from home in 2005, at about the same time that I began studying mindfulness meditation. I was practicing mindful meditation each time I walked to the bathroom throughout the day. I would clear my mind before I began my walk and then with attention to my breath and to each step, I would mindfully walk to the bathroom and go through the process on the toilet with a blank mind. This was so transformative for me because it opened me up to how my everyday actions could be transformed through mindful attention.

The best thing about mindfulness meditation is that you can practice it within your existing daily routines without allocating any additional time to it. Choose one or two routines every day to begin practicing mindfulness meditation with. A daily practice will open your mind to this type of meditation and will bring greater clarity to whatever you are doing.

Meditation can prepare you for your ritual, and can give you greater insight and peace during your daily ritual practice. You can create the intention to meditate mindfully while you are moving through your ritual. In this way, you allow yourself to let go of any doubts, worries or concerns about other things. You allow yourself to fall completely into the ritual mindfully. This is a key to transformative ritual work.

Prayer

Prayer helps form and strengthen a connection to your spirit. Your ritual can include meaningful religious prayer or personal prayer. Religious prayer is a formal prayer that is meant to be repeated. Personal prayer is informal and involves a conversation with your spirit. If you don't have a formal or personal prayer practice, it is easiest to start by finding a prayer that you like, and dedicate a time daily to reading it as you open your heart to the infinite creator of our universe… Explore our growing collection of prayers for inspiration.

Fasting

Fasting is an ancient spiritual practice rooted in the belief in self-discipline and meaningful sacrifice. Christians believe that during fasting, less time is focused on the preparation and consumption of food. This allows for a period of time to pray and develop a closer relationship with your spirit. A food fast gives your body's organs a chance to rest. A media fast includes abstaining from news media, entertainment, information, shopping, email and the Internet. Both types of fasts gives you an opportunity to disengage from the outside world and move into deeper union with your spirit. Before your ritual try to spend time practicing short fasts of media or food. This is because it is best to begin a ritual with a clear mind and body.

For a long time, before I began working with clients doing energy healing work, before I began my first ritual of healing, I would eat a large quantity of food, generally breads and fruit. It became almost a ritual for me to eat before my healings, I had this overwhelming sensation come over me and I would have to eat something, a substantial amount of something, before I began. As I spent time with this craving and questioned it with an open and curious mind, I realized that I was not grounded enough to deliver my healing to my clients. The foods I was eating were helping me to work with the divine light and spiritual realms, but not helping me to bring this healing to others. Slowly and over time, I changed my diet to include more grounding foods like beans and grains. I also now feed myself regularly and plentifully throughout the day, so that I no longer get the craving to eat before I work with a client. Fasting can help you tune into your body more, and your body is your greatest teacher, it will tell you everything you need for this journey. Your body and your mind's greatest wisdom lies deep within, and fasting quiets everything to help you to listen.

Listening to Devotional Music

Many religions use devotional music to heighten feelings of connection to their spirit. In Hinduism, music is a crucial element of the spiritual quest and liturgical ritual. In indigenous South Asian cultures, the world for music, "samgita," described a ritualistic experience that included vocal song, instrumental music, dance, performance and dramatic reenactments. New Age music, Christian music, gospel music, Gregorian chanting and Kirtan are all examples of modern devotional music. You can begin any regular daily ritual with devotional music. Here is my absolute favorite devotional mantra for beginning my day, or ending my day, or any time I need spiritual uplifting.

Each morning I pray this prayer, lighting a candle and welcoming the Earth, the Goddess, and Presence.

Simple Prayer

Today, let this light bless me
With peaceful rain let it bless me
With joyful embrace bless me

Let the vow unto Goddess keep
Wildly and wholly
Spoken and silent
Sleeping and waking

As I unfold Magically inside Her eyes
Let Her fierceness and tenderness hold me
Let Her vastness be undisguised
In all Her ways

Blessed Be

Healing Our Cries
Ritual for Healing Sexual Trauma

Our Shared Story

God Herself, Goddess, Great Mother, Cosmic Mother, she who has many names and no name; has appeared throughout history and through many lenses. In this ritual of healing we will honor and invite God Herself as she appears in Greek pantheon as Hecate1. Getting familiar with Hecate is a life journey, as her mysteries are woven through many faces. She is triple Goddess, great Goddess, and in time evolves into the witch's Goddess. It is important to note, that medieval society transforms her from the Greek's empowered image of divine feminine strength into a hag. Hecate is the uncommon Goddess or the dark Goddess because she symbolizes something that is scary to many. She is death. Death however is not something to be frightened of, but rather to embrace, because it is only through death that we find rebirth and regeneration. This ritual embraces death and the darkness within the Moon to heal our cries.

Hecate is the keeper of the crossroads, the gatekeeper, and navigator. It is she to whom people must seek as they journey with life's cycle of death and rebirth. "It was Hecate whom Demeter turned to after her daughter Persephone had been kidnapped and was seeking clarity in the crisis, and it was Hecate that heard cries as Hades raped Persephone in the Underworld. It was also Hecate that guided Persephone to and from the Underworld to fulfill her annual obligation in the Eleusinian mysteries, thus completing the cycle of the harvest and return to springtime."

This ritual is designed to occur on or around the Dark Moon, a time that magically marks endings. It is important to remember that lunar cycles represent life cycles. As the moon wanes into the sliver of a crescent, the darkness gives birth to new and then from darkness eclipses into light again with the waxing of what will become a bright full moon. As we come to know our lunar cycle, we see it reflected in the tide that give rise to new life, we see it in how bodies menstruate, and we see it in the dance the Moon plays with the Sun giving us season after season.

Aligning this ritual with the Dark Moon naturally aligns with Hecate as she the one who transitions us through life cycles. Hecate however is not a Savioress, or a Deliver of circumstance. That may leave many to think she is cold and unkind. You may ask, why did she not rescue Persephone from Hades? In the Demeter/Persephone creation story, Hecate did not rescue Persephone from her fate. Rather she only helped to facilitate Persephone's transition from one place in her life to another. We do not know what counsel Hecate gave Persephone on that journey from the Underworld, only that she heard her cries and walked with her every year to and from as her constant companion.

This is the lesson! Hecate provides us the key to deliver ourselves by walking with us. She allows us to leave our burden at the gate. She also hears us when we are crying. She hears our suffering, even when our cries are silent to other's ears.

Part of Hecate's wisdom is to help us navigate and understand the cycle of death and regeneration. Often we hear people say, "When he raped me a part of me died." And they are right. This is one ritual of many that allows you to let Hecate transition you from that death to rebirth. We must embrace the fear and find the wisdom rather than be swallowed by the fear and never know the wisdom.

Hecate can also help us to unlock our limitless potential. However to do that we first must look into our darkest self.

Tools:

Lavender Oil
Lush dark-colored fruit of your choosing
Chocolate Candy Bar
One White Seven-Day Candle
A Dark Colored Bowl filled with water
A Heavy Blanket
Tarot Cards or favorite divinatory tool

Ritual Preparation

I invite you to prepare for this ritual in a way that is familiar to your tradition or spiritual practice. For me, I will start with shower where I have filled the tub with some water first and added Epsom salt. This way I can shower and soak my feet at the same time. I will also add a few chamomile tea bags to my foot soak, the cheap kind and just relax into the moment. Please take your time, as this is an evening ritual, please make it about you. I scrub and exfoliate my entire body. I wash away my day, I also was away my expectation of what I think this ritual should be.

While I am in ritual bath, I will have lit some sage so my ritual space is also nicely cleansed in energy. I prefer to work in loose pants and a tank top, barefoot. This ritual feels natural to me preformed on the floor. It can also be done sitting in a chair with a small table in front for the candle. However, I would not do it standing due to the nature of the Invocation.

Personally, I do not cast a circle when working alone. If you do, I invite you to consider this a moment when a circle would be cast. Please use whatever casting feels right to your tradition.

Alignment

Light the White Seven-Day Candle in front of you and enter into a state of meditation until you are centered and still. Counting your breath, actively breathe in peace and breathe out love. Emotive breath work is just that, feelings. There is no right way to breathe in peace or love, just feel the sensation of love and peace, as you understand it.

Focus on being present in this moment. Stay connected with your physical self, your body, breathing in peace. Being present with your emotional self, breathe out love. Being present with your divine self, breathe in peace and as your parts come together breathe out love.
Vision each of your parts whole and complete as source of energy, as they come into alignment, when you are centered, feeling your parts align, open your eye.

Meeting Hecate At The Gate

Does any part of Hecate's story feel familiar? Do you know her? Has she helped you before?

For this Invocation, I find a pillow propped under me provides ease. We want to be able to balance the bowl on our lap, occasionally steadying it with our hands. The eventual goal will be to look into the bowl while chanting and have the ability to see our reflection.

In the process of chanting you may see the face of Hecate mixed in the reflection of the water with your own face or feel her embrace you as if to guide you. Do not be afraid. She has been with you on this journey a very long time whether you are aware or not.

When you are doing this invocation you may cry. You may weep uncontrollably and that is ok. This is why I choose to be seated, rather than standing. Just cry into the bowl, wrapping yourself tightly within the blanket. Remember your breath, breathing in peace and breathing our love. You may also not be able to cry. Do not become frustrated. Instead, remember the breath and keep chanting. Your cries are inside of you, and Hecate hears them even if you do not see them. In time they will come.

To begin, you will recite the invocation looking into the white candle. After you have steadily found your breath and voice with the words, you will begin to slowly recite the invocation looking into the bowl of water. You will repeat the invocation while raising the energy, maintaining the breath. As your energy and voice raises, feel you lower torso expand, and your lower half (your bottom) feel as if it is opening and bearing down, pressing into the pillow or chair, elongate your torso, and neck, breathe deep and raise the energy. Feel Hecate and look deeply into the bowl, breathing in peace, breathing out love...God Herself is around you, Hecate is around you.

You will continue in this fashion through the chanting until you feel you have filled the bowl with energy. This may be minutes or an hour. Remember to breathe. If at any time while chanting you feel yourself loosing the breath, you are to look at the candle. It represents the light that Hecate holds at the gate, like a beacon.

Invocation to Hecate

You listened when he took me
You heard me when I screamed
You rocked me when he left me
You held me in esteem

You stood my silent witness
You navigate my journey still
You walk side by side with me
You are might, strength and will

You listened when he took me
You heard me when I screamed
You rocked me when he left me
You held me in esteem

You gave me voice and power
You taught me to take back the night
You bring me the keys to wisdom

You fill me with power and light

You listened when he took me
You heard me when I screamed
You rocked me when he left me
You held me in esteem

You hear the crying out eternal
You are the keeper at the Gate
You deliver the death of my rape
You bring rebirth in that is my Fate.

You listened when he took me
You heard me when I screamed
You rocked me when he left me
You held me in esteem

You anoint me with your mystery
You the Dark Moon in this release
Deliver me, Divine me,
Make me sacred You
Hecate bring me Peace!

As you come out of the Invocation and return to deep breath, look at the white pure light of the candle. Think on Hecate and on your cries, feeling those cries wash away and into the bowl. Tonight's cries, they need not be with you anymore. Tonight we will offer them to the Dark Moon and request that Hecate take them to the furthest place and release them from us.

Closing
You may find that you want spend some time in reflection before transitioning out of this ritual space and into closing. Most likely you will be tired and you may feel inclined simply to crawl into bed. However it is important to ground yourself, even if you feel drained and instinctively want to just go to bed. Remember you have opened yourself up, invited Hecate into your space, asked her to guild your cries out of your body, heart and soul and into a vessel. It is not only the responsible thing, but also the respectful one that we release that which we have called upon to aide us.

Now let us discharge the contents of the vessel back into earth.

Take your bowl to an open window or door to the outside. Look into the bowl and say out aloud,
"Goddess Hecate, I thank you for hearing my cries and releasing them from me today. Please take them and these tears away with the tonight's Dark Moon."

While pouring the water out into the earth or down the drain visualize those tears and Hecate navigating them away from you.

It is also important to be mindful that Hecate has come into your sacred presence. Offering reverence to her is more than just saying thank you. Consider a ritual offering but also actual actions. First we'll start with your fruit. Plan to feed it back to nature with these words: *"I offer this fruit as a symbol of my devotion to you. I will leave it in my yard or park tonight for one of your night creatures to feast on. I thank you for hearing me, for journeying with me, and your love. Go in Peace and I thank you."*

Also, if you are able, find a way to navigate into someone's life, be it through a youth center, a hotline, or crisis center as a volunteer. The essence of living in communion with God Herself and the faces of Goddess are to make manifest it within you. You too can be like Hecate and help navigate someone through troubled times. Even a simple donation plants a seed in doing Her works.

Before you release the elements and thank God Herself, take a moment and thank yourself!

As above and So below.
Even you, Even I.
All Earth.
All Goddess.
All Sacred.
Enter Into Presence.
Blessed Be.

As I was putting this anthology together it became clearer and clearer that *Alone In Her Presence*, the blog had finally been realized into *Alone In Her Presence* the book, and that a chapter in my life had circled into a new door opening. In the light of my most private need, *Alone* served as an anonymous beacon for learning, and helped prepare me for the larger journey ahead, that of coming into presence.

The presence has not been easy.

After I received that phone call from the Pagan elder I wrote about in the beginning of this book. within what felt like a flash, I was the center of so much light and magic that I did not have the tools to handle it. Was I 'wishfully thinking' while assuming I 'knew' the Goddess more intimately than I did? Who knows exactly, but my ability to articulate my feelings stifled, to self regulate my frustrations blossomed, and in the vortex of 'notoriety' I felt invisible and unheard. Weird, I know, but true.

Like the Horned God, I 'died' into darkness. What was evident to me was that while I was, and am, certainly immanent, I was not embodied within my own body. My mind truly was greater than the sum of my parts. I left the web of my online Pagan persona and took refuge in Tantric yoga practice, invoked Kali, and began to feel my body for the first time. In this process of feeling deeply and exploring who I truly was, I had to let go of what I thought I needed and wanted to be. I stopped trying to be Pagan, I ended a long-term relationship, I turned off the movie in my mind that I was calling "Dharma Pagan" and stopped trying to be everything to everyone, and instead invited true empowered surrender.

Magic- I know it. My cards always turning and talking to the trees continued. My "primitive" candle gazing and simple rituals never stopped. But what I realized in this profound moment of introspection was that I have a monogamous relationship with Goddess and in the polarity that is effervescent energy, I am the God form to Her. Digging deeper into yoga, I came to know my physical body and fall in love with it as a manifestation of divinity. For the first time, my body, mind, and spirit came into alignment and then the Goddess truly spoke to me. I came to know (and not just feel) that Her's is the love unwavering that flows in, among and around me and that was palpable in it's authentic realness. This with my daily practice of yoga, I came back to my practice of creating ritual and performing them. Back to doing magic, in the purest and most simple form. The form that has been with me from the beginning and resulted in desire. I returned to the Light of Presence.

I also spent time watching those within my pagan circle as I journeyed into alignment with my sense of self and body back into fruition. Those who I love so dearly, many seemed to go through life changes. I watched Teo turn into Christianity. I light a candle on my altar nightly for him because when we invoke patriarchy's God it becomes harder to feel the Great Mother. Through all this, there is my beloved mentor and teacher Yeshe Rabbit. Her love, spaciousness, forgiveness and support, ever present. Her gift of magic pure and true. Her light upon my journey unwavering.

What I have come to realize is that I needed the internal perspective in order to begin the next chapter. It was ok to step away from the flame of being known. It became clear that I am is interested in is wisdom, and seeking the magic in the ordinary and falling in love with extraordinary truth that is found in immanent divinity. I continue to endeavor that the wisdom I seek to find and share here will bring hope, peace, and harmony to others. That the truth that knowing Goddess is all we ever need, will be consumed by everyone.

As I release *Alone In Her Presence*, I too, honor everything that She was in cultivating the light of presence. I hope that these poems and stories have inspired you, have filled your heart and touched your soul. Perhaps they have offered you a deeper connection to yourself, or something more, an opening to know Goddess.

Whether you are alone or among many, take a moment for presence. This moment, this journey and this life in magic, is perfect as is.

Erick DuPree

Writer • Magic Maker • Wisdom Seeker

Erick holds a Masters in Comparative Literature from Queen's University, and is former Religious Educator for the historic Arlington Street Church: Boston under mentor Rev. Kim K Crawford Harvie. His studies in magic include working within a Reclaiming Collective, Soul Work with T. Thorn Coyle, The Origins of Tantra with Dr. Douglas Brooks, and Dharma Paganism with current teacher Yeshe Rabbit Matthews.

As writer, he has contributed to numerous anthologies including *Rooted in the Body Seeking the Soul* and *Bringing Race to the Table: An Exploration of Racism in the Pagan Community*. He is author of *Universally Unique: Homilies, Lessons, and Lore* (2010 Chalice Press), and forthcoming books, T*he Hero Within: Reframing Masculinity with Paganism's Gods* and the anthology *Finding Masculine in Goddess' Spiral: Men in Ritual, Community and Service to the Goddess*, both by Immanion Press.

Learn more about Erick at www.erickdupree.com

www.ingramcontent.com/pod-product-compliance
Lightning Source LLC
Chambersburg PA
CBHW060203050426
42446CB00013B/2974